FANTASTIC FACTS ABOUT

AUSTRALIA'S REMARKABLE PLACES

FRANCES PAYNE

REDBACK publishing

Redback Publishing
Suite 6, 13a Narabang Way,
Belrose NSW 2085
Australia

www.redbackpublishing.com
orders@redbackpublishing.com

Reprinted 2025

978-1-922322-73-9

Author: Frances Payne
Editor: Caroline Thomas
Designer: Redback Publishing

Originated by Redback Publishing

Acknowledgements
Abbreviations: l—left, r—right, b—bottom, t—top, c—centre, m—middle
We would like to thank the following for permission to reproduce photographs: (Images © shutterstock)
P16m Great Artesian Basin, by Tentotwo [CC BY-SA 3.0 (https://creativecommons.org/licenses/by-sa/3.0)] via Wikimedia Commons, p18m The Fort - West Wallabi Island by Rupert Gerritsen [CC BY-SA 3.0 (https://creativecommons.org/licenses/by-sa/3.0)], via Wikimedia Commons, p18b Elizabeth Farm-3 by Sardaka (talk) 06:15, 23 January 2013 (UTC) [CC BY 3.0 (https://creativecommons.org/licenses/by/3.0)], via Wikimedia Commons, p19b Section of The Old Great North Road by Conollyb [CC BY-SA 3.0 (https://creativecommons.org/licenses/by-sa/3.0)], via Wikimedia Commons, p21b Overland telegraph construction 1872, National Archives of Australia [Public domain],p23t Anbangbang gallery Mimi rock art cropped, Photo by and ©2002 Dustin M. Ramsey (Kralizec!) [CC BY-SA 2.5 (https://creativecommons.org/licenses/by-sa/2.5)], via Wikimedia Commons, p26t Coober Pedy Jewellery shop by Lodo27, [CC BY-SA 3.0 (https://creativecommons.org/licenses/by-sa/3.0)], via Wikimedia, p27m One of the Batavia mutiny (1629) victims, excavated on Beacon Island and now displayed at Fremantle Shipwreck Museum by Guy de la Bedoyere [CC BY-SA 4.0 (https://creativecommons.org/licenses/by-sa/4.0)], via Wikimedia Commons, p28lt The melancholy loss of HMS Sirius off Norfolk Island March 19th 1790, by George Raper [Public Domain], p28t Xanthe Rivett, Archaeologist Kieran Hosty behind Anchor from HMCS Mermaid, 2009, courtesy Silentworld Foundation, p28m NIMAA members snorkelling on the last Sirius anchor still on the sea floor, http://norfolkislandmuseum.blogspot.com/2014/03/protecting-hms-sirius-wrecksite-and-her.html [Public domain], p28b S.S. Yongala, State Library Victoria [Public domain], p28b HMAS Australia by E. A. Bradford, State Library Victoria [Public domain], p29tl USS-Peary-DD226 by U.S. Navy [Public domain], p29rt HMAS Sydney 1941, Fox photos [Public domain], via Wikipedia Commons, p29b The wreck of the Centaur, 1943, Brisbane City Council Library [Public domain].

NATIONAL LIBRARY OF AUSTRALIA

A catalogue record for this book is available from the National Library of Australia

CONTENTS

The Endless Outback

MILLIONS OF YEARS OLD

The Australian Outback is a term that refers to the enormous deserts and grasslands that cover most of the interior parts of the continent. This is a mainly flat landscape which is very ancient. Some parts of the Outback have barely changed over millions of years. The Outback's low human population has contributed to it remaining one of the Earth's great unspoiled expanses of land.

AWASH WITH WATER

Although we tend to imagine the Outback being all dry deserts, this is not the case. Massive areas are savannahs, which means they are covered with grasses and bushes. When the rain comes in the northern wet season, the savannahs are awash with water.

DESERT TOURISM

Australia's Outback is a tourist attraction. People are fascinated by deserts, and they can visit them in Australia while still being just a short plane ride away from a five-star hotel and all its relaxing luxuries. Cultural tourism in the Outback attracts visitors who are eager to find out about the Indigenous people who have retained their culture for thousands of years, longer than any other human community.

BEYOND THE BLACK STUMP

When tourists ask how to get to the Outback, locals will tell them it's "Beyond the black stump!" This mythical stump is supposedly an old, burnt tree somewhere in the Outback, but exactly where is a mystery. A number of places claim they have the original black stump, including Blackall in Queensland, and Coolah in New South Wales.

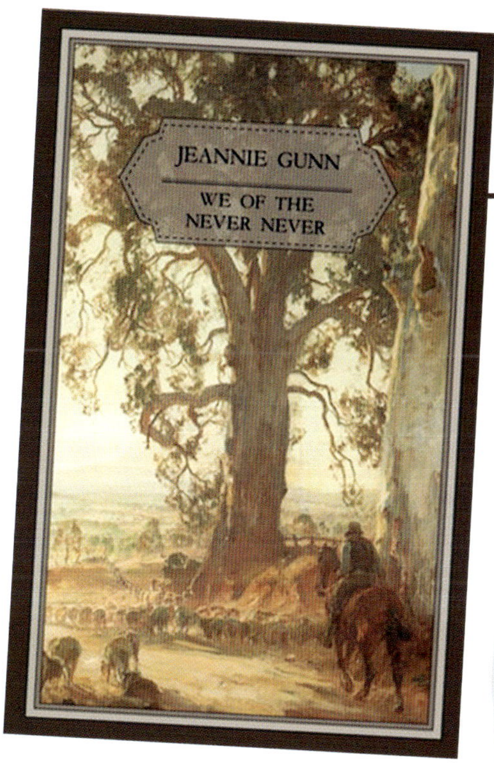

THE NEVER NEVER

Jeannie Gunn's book *We of the Never Never* first appeared in 1908, and soon became a bestseller. It is a novel based on the author's own life amongst the Indigenous people of the Northern Territory. Gunn did not invent the term Never Never, which was in use years before, but it was her book that thrust the term into popular usage around Australia as a way to describe the Outback.

BIG EVERYTHING

Australia is the home of big statues of just about anything. Travellers to country towns will find statues of big animals, big fruit and lots of other symbols of the area they are visiting. Some of the statues are made of fibreglass, while others are moulded metal. The big things of Australia are a humorous way of promoting towns and regions, and they make a great background for holiday photos.

The Angry Earth

VOLCANOES

A string of volcanoes stretches along the east coast of Australia. Don't worry, they are all either dormant or extinct. These volcanoes erupted during a time when the tectonic plate on which Australia sits was moving across a hot-spot deep under the surface. Australia has now moved on, and volcanic eruptions on the mainland are very unlikely.

There are still active volcanoes in Australia, but they are not on the mainland. They are on Heard Island and the McDonald Islands, located in the stormy waters between Australia and Antarctica.

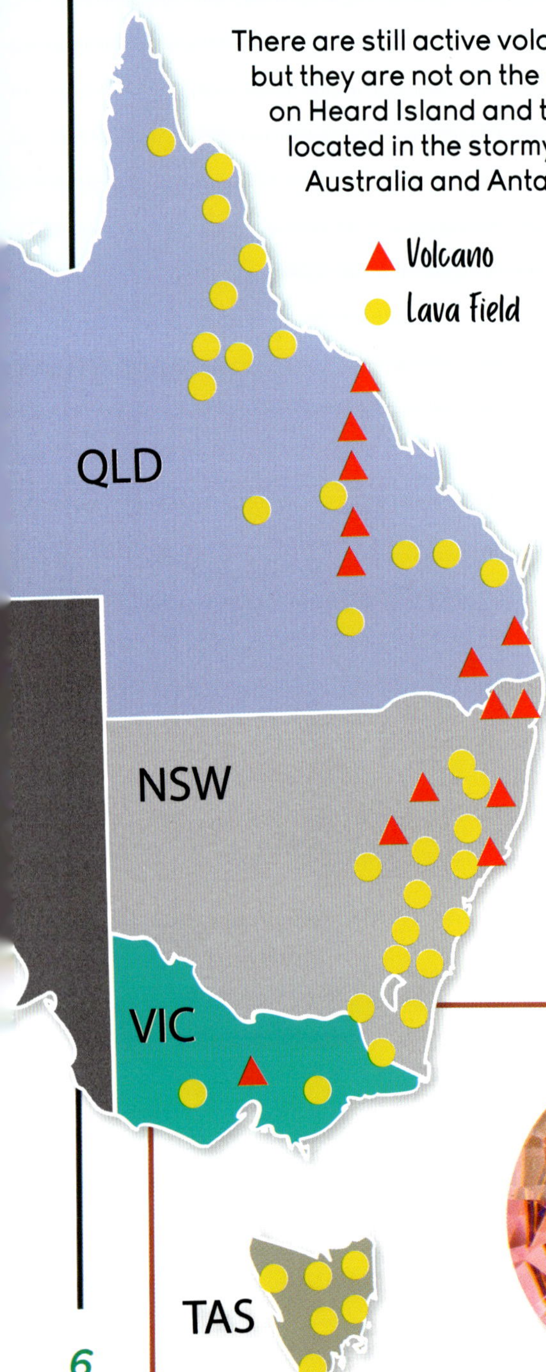

A few of the volcanoes to look out for as you travel around Australia:

- **New South Wales**
  Mount Warning, The Breadknife, Mount Kaputar, Mount Canobolas.
- **Queensland**
  Glass House Mountains, Murray Island, Mount Fox.
- **South Australia**
  Mount Gambier, Mount Schank.
- **Tasmania**
  Table Cape, The Nut.
- **Victoria**
  Mount Elephant, Tower Hill, Mount Napier, Mount Leura, Mount Noorat, Mount Buninyong, Mount Warrenheip.

DIAMONDS AND VOLCANOES

How could a beautiful, cold diamond ring be connected with an angry, hot volcano? The rare pink diamonds from the Argyle Mine in Western Australia are extracted from a lava flow that came out of an unbelievably hot volcano millions of years ago.

METEOR CRATERS

At various times throughout Earth's history, large meteors have crashed into Australia, leaving mighty craters. Along the east coast, where there has been a lot of volcanic activity and mountain building, the remains of these craters are difficult to see. In contrast, in the untouched Outback, shockingly huge craters still exist.

Craters in Western Australia

- **Hickman Crater, WA**
  260 metres wide.
- **Woodleigh Crater, WA**
  Although now buried under sedimentary rocks, this crater may be over 60 kilometres wide. The site contains deposits of reidite, an extremely rare mineral that only exists on Earth at places where meteors have fallen.
- **Wolfe Creek Crater, WA**
  900 metres wide.

Craters in the Northern Territory

- **Gosse's Bluff, NT**
  Dated to over a hundred million years old. Erosion has reduced the size of this crater from twenty-two to five kilometres wide.
- **Henbury Craters, NT**
  A group of small craters that are only a few thousand years old.
- **Boxhole Crater, NT**
  175 metres wide.

Living on Ancient Land

NULLARBOR PLAIN

One of the driest places in Australia was once just the opposite. The Nullarbor Plain on Australia's southern coast used to be at the bottom of an ocean. The limestone that makes the surface land of the Nullarbor so dry was formed millions of years ago by tiny marine organisms. When they died, their bodies dropped to the sea floor and compacted together to form limestone. Although the surface of the Nullarbor is dry, beneath it are networks of caves, many containing pools of underground water.

NEARLY AS OLD AS THE EARTH

There are parts of Australia that are almost unchanged since planet Earth formed, four and a half billion years ago. The rocks of the Pilbara region in the north of Western Australia are about three and half billion years old. While other parts of the world experienced volcanic activity that changed the surface, the Pilbara rocks have stayed almost the same. As the mighty continental plates drifted around the globe, the rocks of the Pilbara moved with them, eventually ending up where they are now.

LONGEST PLACE NAME

There really is a place in Australia called Mamungkukumpurangkuntjunya Hill. It is in South Australia and the name is a Pitjantjatjara word.

Gondwana

Australian Protea

African Protea

TAKE A STEP INTO AFRICA, INDIA AND ANTARCTICA

Before people knew anything about the movement of land across the surface of the Earth in the process called tectonics, they found it difficult to explain how so many plants that grow in Africa are similar to ones that grow in Australia. The reason is that the two land masses were once connected as part of the great ancient continent called Gondwana. Sixty-five million years ago, this land mass began to split up and Australia slowly drifted away to where it is now.

Look at these pictures of proteas from Australia and from Africa. They look the same, don't they?

WE'RE ON THE MOVE!

Australians are all travelling north whether we like it or not. Our continent sits on a huge continental plate that is drifting northeast at a rate of seven centimetres each year. In December 2017, the GPS coordinates of places in Australia were all about two metres wrong because the continent had moved that far since the coordinates were last set in the 1990s. Geoscience Australia has set us right though, and now the various software systems that rely on precise locations have the exact information they need.

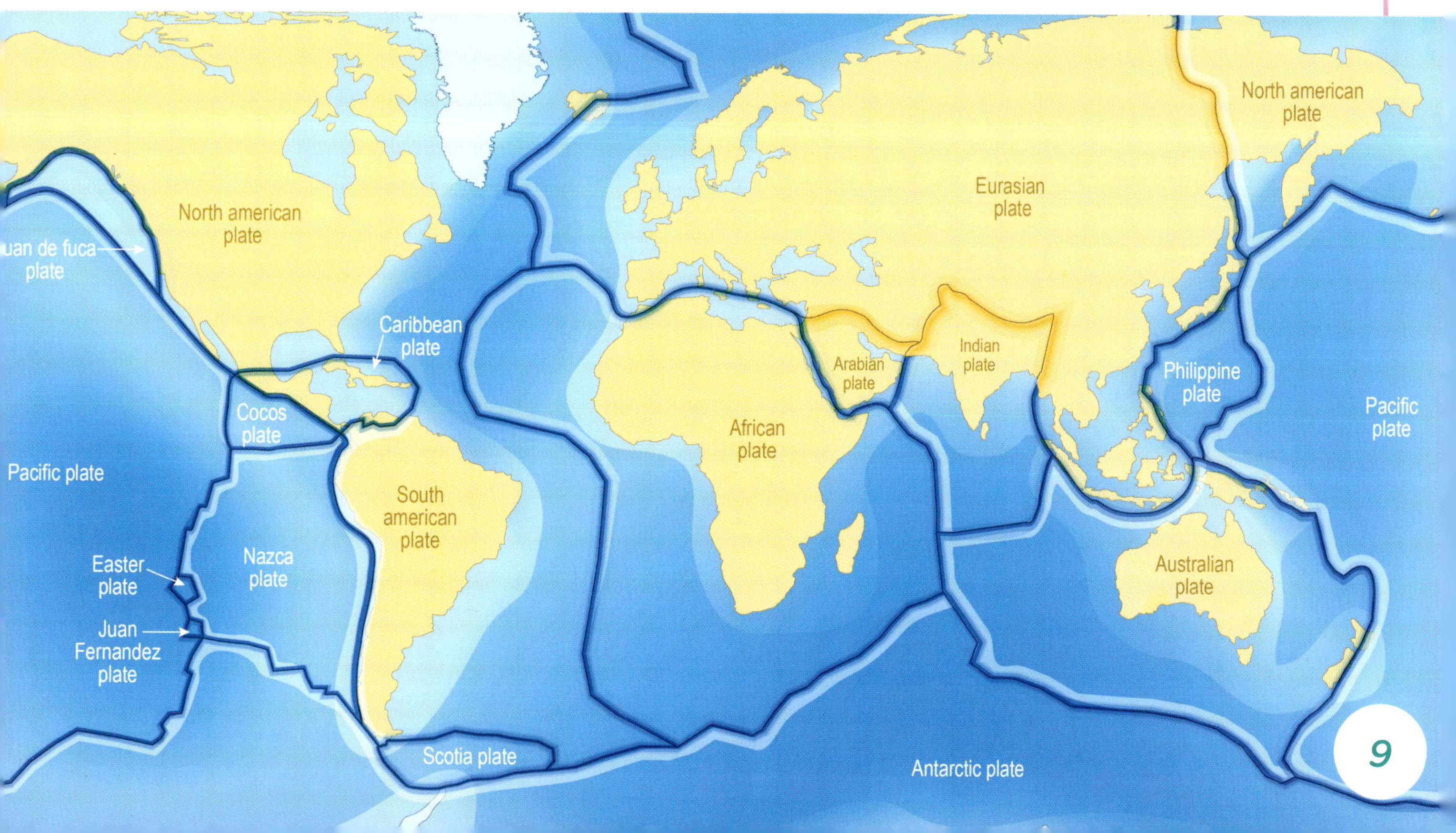

The Last Ice Age

THE CONTINENT USED TO BE BIGGER

Before the end of the last Ice Age, about 10,000 years ago, the continent of Australia used to be much bigger. Papua New Guinea and Tasmania were both joined to the mainland by land bridges, and the east coast extended a long way out into what is now the ocean. Rising sea levels, caused by the melting of the ice caps, flooded the low-lying land connections. This left Australia in the shape we recognise as our country today.

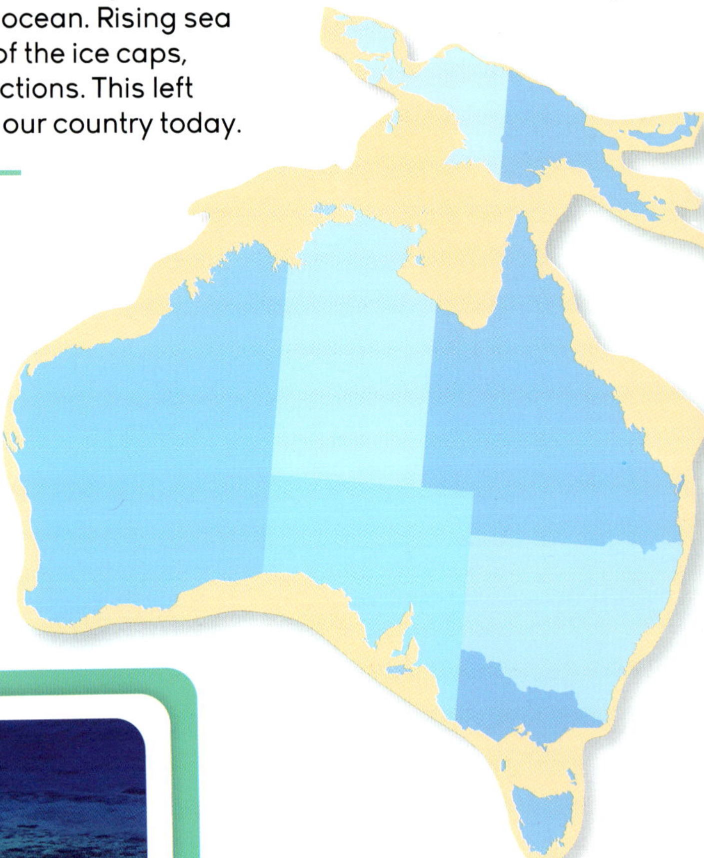

TASMANIA

When human beings first arrived in Australia from the north, at least 65,000 years ago, they took a few thousand years to cross the land and reach Australia's southern extremity. When sea levels were lower than today, these people reached Tasmania by walking across dry land, or paddling their canoes over shallow water. The ending of the last Ice Age caused sea levels to rise, resulting in the separation of the island of Tasmania.

GREAT BARRIER REEF

During the last Ice Age, the more shallow parts of the Great Barrier Reef were dry land. The local Indigenous people have stories preserved in their Dreamings about the time when the sea used to be dry land.

WHAT CAUSED THE LAST ICE AGE?

So much of Australia's prehistoric past was shaped by the last Ice Age that it is interesting to know why it occurred and why it ended.

Earth has experienced a number of Ice Ages since it formed from stardust 4.6 billion years ago. The most recent Ice Age ended about 10,000 years ago, when glaciers and ice at the poles melted, raising sea levels all around the world.

The reason for the changing temperature of the Earth's climate is not really clear, but it may have been due to a combination of factors. These include different energy levels coming from the Sun, the Earth's natural wobble making its orbit different, and the effect of geological events that release heat from the centre of the Earth, or that throw volcanic dust into the atmosphere, cooling the temperature on the surface.

The Earth is currently in an interglacial age, which means that we are living in a period between the last Ice Age and the next one. The difference now is that humans are affecting the Earth's climate in ways that never happened before. No-one knows for certain what effect this could have on future Ice Ages.

Unusual Plants in Australia

Some places are special because of what grows there, either naturally or through the hard work of farmers.

OPIUM BY THE TRUCKLOAD

Tasmania is one of the world's main sources of legal, medical grade opium. Opium comes from the opium poppy and is used to make drugs for the treatment of severe pain.

THE SECRET FOREST OF WOLLEMI PINES

Hidden deep in the forests of the Blue Mountains in New South Wales are the descendants of a unique tree that grew when dinosaurs roamed the area, around 100 million years ago. The Wollemi Pine was only discovered in 1994. Wollemi Pines are now planted as garden trees, although they can grow to be extremely large. People who want a tree from the Age of the Dinosaurs in their garden need to be sure they have enough room for it to grow safely.

LEAVES ONLY FALL IN TASMANIA

Australia has only a tiny number of native trees that lose their leaves, unlike European countries where the display of red and orange leaves in the autumn is sung about in songs, and written about in poems and stories. The only Australian tree to put on this display is the beech tree in Tasmania. Its leaves turn orange then drop in preparation for the cold winter. There is also another tree that loses its leaves, but this one lives in the desert. It's the boab or bottle tree - the one with the fat trunk. It loses its leaves just before the hot, dry season. This adaptation stops water being lost through transpiration from its leaves during a time when there will be no rain to keep the tree alive.

Lots of Sand

Sand defines an unexpectedly large number of places throughout Australia. While this at first seems to be just an inexplicable oddity, the reasons for it become clear when we think about the extreme age of the Australian continent. Sand can result when rocks are subjected to weathering over millennia. Sand can also build up when wind and water currents pile it into hills or onto shores over long periods of time when there has been no volcanic or geological activity to interrupt the process.

THE RED CENTRE

Anyone who has flown in an aeroplane across the middle of Australia will have looked down and seen red sand below for hours. The sand is red because part of it comes from rocks that have a large amount of hematite in them. Hematite is iron ore and its mining and export is one of Australia's largest industries.

SAND ISLANDS

The largest sand islands in the world are all in Australia. They are Fraser Island, Moreton Island, North Stradbroke Island and Bribie Island, all in Queensland. Sand islands form when sand is blown and washed onto an area, and plants then stabilise the sand. Over many thousands of years, soil builds up and a whole plant community develops.

NINETY MILE BEACH

Ninety Mile Beach in Victoria is one of the longest beaches in the world.

Must - See Lakes in Australia

PINK LAKES

Lake Hillier in Western Australia is a bright pink lake. The colour is caused by algae in the water. Lake Hillier is on Middle Island so it is not easy to get to or to see. Flying over it gives people the best view, as the pink contrasts sharply with the blue of the nearby ocean. Western Australia has another pink lake as well. It is called, well, Pink Lake! The degree of its pinkness varies; possibly due to the salinity of its water.

LAKE ARGYLE

Lake Argyle in Western Australia was created as a result of a dam built for the Ord River Irrigation Scheme. The lake holds more water than Sydney Harbour. Lake Argyle is both a source of fresh water for irrigation and a water sports location for visitors, but there are also thousands of freshwater crocodiles living in it. Although they are not as aggressive as the 'salties', freshwater crocodiles are still best avoided if possible.

LAKE COOTAPATAMBA

Lake Cootapatamba is the highest lake in Australia, at 2,048 metres above sea level. It was formed by glacial activity and is only a short distance from the summit of Mount Kosciuszko.

LAKE PEDDER and LAKE GORDON

Lake Pedder in Tasmania was the focus of a fierce protest by environmentalists in the 1970s. They tried to stop the government damming the Gordon River to flood the wilderness areas. The protesters failed to save the original, smaller Lake Pedder from flooding, but their protests led to the growth of the green movement in Australian politics. Despite the flooding of Lake Pedder, the surrounding wilderness is dense, beautiful and unspoiled.

LAKE MUNGO

No longer water-filled, the stark, desert landscape of Lake Mungo was once a beautiful wetland. Fifty thousand years ago, trees and bushland grew around lakes that were full of fish. The remains of Mungo Lady and Mungo Man were found buried beneath the sand. They lived over 40,000 years ago, making them some of the oldest human remains found worldwide. Mungo National Park and Lake Mungo are in New South Wales.

Water in Strange Places

RIVERS AND LAKES HIDDEN IN CAVES

The Jenolan Caves in New South Wales are one of Australia's most beautiful cave systems, and they attract thousands of tourists every year. The caves they visit are well-lit and have stairs and hand rails, but these are only a tiny proportion of the whole underground cave system. There are many more to discover.

The Jenolan Caves exist because the limestone which forms them was once underneath a warm sea. Millions of years ago, tiny sea creatures died and left their little skeletons on the seabed. These later formed limestone. When the seabed became land, freshwater filtering through the limestone created tunnels and underground lakes, as well as forming the stalactites and stalagmites in the caves.

EROMANGA SEA IN THE MIDDLE OF AUSTRALIA

In the early 1800s, there was a persistent idea amongst the colonists that there must be a mighty sea in the middle of Australia. They observed many rivers flowing in a westerly direction and believed they must all empty into something. In fact, the rivers turn and end up with their mouths reaching the ocean. Strangely, there did used to be a sea in the centre of Australia. Millions of years before there were any human beings there, the centre of Australia was an inland sea surrounded by islands of higher land. Scientists have named it the Eromanga Sea.

The Great Artesian Basin is a remnant of the inland Eromanga Sea

VAST SEA UNDER THE GROUND

Deep beneath the dry deserts, there is a surprising resource. Lots of water! The water is held in artesian basins, and Indigenous people have known about them for thousands of years. Some of the Indigenous artwork from people of the desert nations uses symbols that show where the underground water rises naturally to the surface as springs. Mining, industry and farming all use the artesian waters by digging bores deep into the rock and pumping water to the surface. The Great Artesian Basin lies beneath 20% of Australia. Some of its underground water is millions of years old.

How Long Before They Fall Down?

TWELVE APOSTLES

In the ocean beside the Great Ocean Road, on Victoria's coast, there used to be nine large rock stacks called The Twelve Apostles. They have been a major tourist attraction for many years. One of the nine rocks collapsed into the sea in 2005. This was an unexpected event, and led people to wonder when the next Apostle will fall.

WEDDING CAKE ROCK

Looking like a huge piece of cake, this rock is on the New South Wales coast near Bundeena. Fenced off to protect the public, the rock sits precariously beside the ocean. No-one knows exactly when, but it will collapse into the waves one day soon.

KARLU KARLU / DEVILS MARBLES

Karlu Karlu / Devils Marbles are a collection of large boulders, some of them six metres wide. They sit on a plain in the Northern Territory and many are stacked one on top of another. They were formed by the erosion of layers of rock, leaving rounded boulder shapes scattered across the landscape.

Oldest Structures in Australia

WHERE? Barwon River, Brewarrina, New South Wales

WHAT? Australian Indigenous people built these fish traps out of stones. The structures formed a group of pools in which trapped fish were easy to catch.

BUILT at least hundreds of years ago and perhaps thousands, but no-one knows for sure.

BUILT in the 1600s

WHERE? West Wallabi Island, off the coast of Western Australia

WHAT? The remains of a roughly built stone fort are all that is left of the defences raised by the survivors of a shipwreck. When the Dutch East India Company ship Batavia sank in 1629, survivors broke into two groups who fought with each other. One group on the island built the stone fort to protect themselves from the others.

WHERE? Rosehill, Sydney, New South Wales

WHAT? The farmhouse known as Elizabeth Farm includes a structure dating from 1793. This makes it Australia's oldest surviving house and a rare example of colonial architecture. The building is now a house museum.

BUILT in 1793

BUILT from 1799 onwards

WHERE? Parramatta, New South Wales

WHAT? Government House in Parramatta Park is the oldest public building still standing in Australia. It is now a house museum set within a whole historic precinct. Stand on its front porch and you can imagine being there over two hundred years ago.

WHERE? Hobart, Tasmania

WHAT? The Commissariat Store is the oldest surviving public building in Tasmania. Its original purpose was to store food for the colonists to prevent them from starving before they had a chance to grow crops to feed themselves. Living off the land using local produce was not an option. Many of the convicts and settlers had come from cities and towns and they had no idea about farming. They also feared eating anything unusual from the strange new land they had come to.

WHERE? The Rocks, Sydney, New South Wales

WHAT? Cadmans Cottage is now right in the heart of Sydney's historic tourist area. In 1816 it was the home of a government official.

WHERE? Coal River at Richmond, Tasmania

WHAT? The Richmond Bridge over the Coal River is the oldest surviving large stone arch bridge in Australia. The bridge is now protected with a bitumen road that carries cars across it every day.

WHERE? Sydney to the Hunter Valley, New South Wales

WHAT? The Old Great North Road was a large engineering project undertaken by the early colonial government, and built by convict workers. Parts of it still exist in their original condition and include bridges and high walls all made from cut sandstone. Today, a road of this length and difficulty would involve the use of heavy machinery, with prefabricated sections being brought in from long distances away. The construction of such a road during the early colonial era was an outstanding achievement.

Engineering Wonders

PYRAMID IN CANBERRA

Look at the huge flagpole on top of Parliament House and imagine it as the top of a pyramid. In fact, this is just what it is meant to look like. The designers of the new Parliament House tried to keep to Walter Burley Griffin's vision, which was to have a pyramid shaped building on the top of Capital Hill. Placing Australia's parliament inside a pyramid was not considered appropriate, but the flagpole on top suggests the bare outline of what could have been.

WHAT'S UNDER THE SYDNEY OPERA HOUSE?

Like a swan gliding serenely over the surface of the water, while its feet are paddling furiously underneath, the beautiful Sydney Opera House also has machinery underneath it that keeps the building functioning. Beneath the white sails there is a massive engineering wonder! Thirty-five kilometres of pipes draw sea water from the harbour to power both the heating and air conditioning, to keep people and precious musical instruments at just the right temperature all year round.

SYDNEY HARBOUR BRIDGE

The Sydney Harbour Bridge opened in 1932. It is the highest steel arch bridge in the world, but not the longest, and it takes pride of place when Australians talk about their iconic buildings and structures. Built during the Great Depression, the construction ended up feeding and housing the families of hundreds of men who would otherwise have been unemployed. Unfortunately, a number of the workers died while building it.

MOVING MIGHTY RIVERS

Snowy Mountains Scheme

Australia's post World War II population boom meant that growing cities needed a better electricity supply and water for irrigation west of the Great Dividing Range. The Snowy Mountains Scheme was designed to meet these demands for power and water. Completed in 1974, the Scheme dammed rivers in the Australian Southern Alps, and used their falling water to generate power. It also diverted water falling in the mountains, stopping it from flowing east to the coast, and sent it westward instead to supply water to towns and farms.

ADELAIDE TO DARWIN RAILWAY TOOK 126 YEARS TO BUILD

Commuters around Australia's cities often complain about the time it takes for roadwork to be finished, but the record for the time taken to complete a piece of transport infrastructure has to be held by the Adelaide to Darwin railway line. At nearly 3,000 kilometres long, it traverses some of the most remote parts of the continent. Begun in 1878, the line finally reached Darwin in 2004.

... BUT THE ADELAIDE TO DARWIN TELEGRAPH LINE ONLY TOOK TWO YEARS

Built only eighty-four years after settlement, the Adelaide to Darwin Overland Telegraph Line was an engineering wonder of its time. The people who constructed it had to be more than builders and surveyors. They were explorers as well. The telegraph line was vitally important because it connected Australia by telegraph to the rest of the world for the first time. This happened using Morse Code sent along the telegraph lines laid from England to Java, in Indonesia, and then to Darwin.

Aboriginal Sacred Sites

WHAT ARE SACRED SITES?

For the Australian Aboriginal people, a sacred site is a place where the ancestors have left their mark on the land – a burial site, a place where people have died or a place with Dreaming significance. The Dreaming is a difficult concept for non-Indigenous people to understand. It encompasses all of time – the past, present and future. The creation spirits exist in The Dreamtime, and Aboriginal people honour them by caring for the land and its waterways, by following the instructions they left behind, and through ceremonies and songs.

ULURU

Uluru is a sacred rock for the local Anangu Aboriginal people. The red dome we can see above the surface of the surrounding desert is only the tip of the whole rock, which extends for kilometres straight down beneath the ground.

WATER

Rivers, billabongs and lakes are special places because they were left behind when creation ancestors travelled across the land. Each Australian Aboriginal nation has its own creation Dreaming, but the Rainbow Serpent appears in many of them as the maker of waterways.

ROCK ART

There is Aboriginal rock art throughout Australia, but the oldest known paintings are in Arnhem Land in the Northern Territory. This art is up to 28,000 years old, making it some of the oldest art in the world. The descendants of the artists still care for the art and can claim an unbroken connection with their ancient ancestors.

KATA TJUTA

Kata Tjuta in the Northern Territory is a group of enormous red rocks, a few kilometres from Uluru. The area is a sacred men's site for the local Anangu Aboriginal people. Geologists estimate that the Kata Tjuta rocks are 500 million years old, while the Anangu confirm they were created during the Dreaming.

VISITORS TO SACRED SITES

Non-Indigenous people who are visiting Aboriginal sacred sites need to behave respectfully. In popular tourist areas, there are often Indigenous rangers or guides to give advice on the places that can be visited and the customs that should be followed. Some sites are for women only to visit and see, while others are just for men.

Ghost Towns

Australia's ghost towns are not inhabited by ghosts. The term refers to a settlement that has been abandoned as people moved away.

A bustling township can turn into a ghost town as the result of a variety of events. It may have been too difficult for people to grow food or find water, the desert sands may have taken over, or a mining town might have closed when the mine became no longer profitable to operate. In times of drought, farmers may have to leave their farms to find work elsewhere. Nearby towns then begin to close down, as shops, schools and churches no longer have any local people to use them.

YERRANDERIE, NEW SOUTH WALES

Nestled deep within the Burragorang forests, Yerranderie is a complete village left behind by its former residents when the local silver mine closed. Once home to 2,000 people, the town is now deserted. It is managed by the National Parks and Wildlife Service.

EUCLA, WESTERN AUSTRALIA

Located on the Nullarbor Plain, Eucla once had its own jetty, and it was an important telegraph relay station. The telegraph buildings are now partially covered with sand. The desert took over when rabbits destroyed much of the town's surrounding vegetation and most of the people left. The jetty is now a disused relic of a former time, when the delivery of food and supplies for Eucla's population depended on boats. Eucla is now a tiny settlement providing services for travellers driving across the Nullarbor Plain.

FARINA, SOUTH AUSTRALIA

In 1876, a couple of hopeful surveyors laid out a township at Farina, thinking it was a good spot for a new settlement that would house over 400 families. The desert was relentless though, and would never have allowed people to settle there. With no water for people, livestock or irrigation, Farina's stone buildings were left to crumble, and its few residents moved on.

WALHALLA, VICTORIA

Walhalla is an historic Gold Rush township dating from the 1860s. It had a population of thousands around that time, but this had reduced to just a few people by the early 2000s. The town has now become a tourist location where visitors go to look around an old gold mining town, set within beautiful forest surroundings.

WADDAMANA, TASMANIA

Waddamana is a different sort of ghost town. Its remaining buildings reveal the early history of the hydro-electric power industry in Tasmania, and how the local workers used to live.

KURIDALA, QUEENSLAND

Kuridala was a copper mining town which had 1,500 residents back in 1913. The closure of the mine started the decline of the town, which once had its own movie theatre, hotels, a hospital and a courthouse. Very little remains, except for some of the mine's rusting equipment and the foundations of town buildings.

ARLTUNGA, NORTHERN TERRITORY

The Arltunga Historical Reserve is about 110 kilometres east of Alice Springs. The gold mining town of Arltunga was one of the earliest European settlements in Central Australia, and the area is now well signposted for visitors. Once the gold ran out, most of the settlers moved on, leaving their buildings to crumble in the desert.

Unusual Places to Live

UNDERGROUND HOMES

Coober Pedy in South Australia reaches such high temperatures in summer that the locals have gone underground. By digging their homes, hotels and shops out of the rock, people manage to live in comfortable surroundings while the surface above is baking. Most of the cave dwelling residents are opal miners.

White Cliffs in New South Wales is another town of underground cave homes.

HOUSEBOATS

Living an idyllic lifestyle on a houseboat is entirely possible on the Murray River in eastern Australia. Although usually enjoyed just for holidays, houseboats are not rare and some people live on them permanently.

BOAB TREES

Boab trees grow hugely fat trunks that become hollow in the middle as the tree ages. At Wyndham in Western Australia there is a boab called the Wyndham Prison Tree. Whether it was ever used as a prison is disputed, but there is certainly space inside for it to have been used for such a purpose. Elsewhere throughout the dry expanses of Australia, the hollow middle of boabs have often been used as places for humans to escape from the fierce sun outside.

Shipwrecks

Being an island nation, Australia is surrounded by shipwrecks. They date from the time when world explorers first ventured into the southern oceans, up until colonial and recent eras. The shipwrecks in Australian waters are a combination of navigation hazards, precious historical sites, places of solemn significance and places where divers can explore the marine life that takes over when a ship sinks to the bottom of the ocean.

There are thousands of shipwrecks off the Australian coast and in harbours and other waterways. Many are still waiting to be explored.

WRECKS OF DUTCH EAST INDIA COMPANY SHIPS

Batavia

- A Dutch East India Company ship. Wrecked in 1629 off the coast of Western Australia.
- What followed the wreck is a terrible tale of murder and mutiny.

Zuytdorp

- A Dutch East India Company ship.
- Wrecked in 1712 off the coast of Western Australia.
- Its cargo of silver and other treasures lay untouched until the wreck was discovered in the mid 1900s.

WRECKS OF COLONIAL SHIPS (AFTER 1788)

HMS Sirius

- A flagship of the First Fleet.
- Wrecked off the coast of Norfolk Island in 1790.
- After bringing the first convicts to Australia, the role of HMS Sirius was to collect food from other countries and bring it back to the starving new settlement.
- Its loss led to further hunger and distress for the little colony at Sydney Cove.

HMS Pandora

- A Royal Navy ship whose mission was to search for the crew and mutineers of HMS Bounty.
- Wrecked on the Great Barrier Reef in 1791.

HMCS Mermaid

- Used to undertake some of the first surveys of the Australian coastline, HM Colonial Schooner Mermaid was wrecked in 1829 off Cairns.

Hive

- A convict transport ship.
- Wrecked in Wreck Bay, New South Wales in 1835.

Loch Ard

- A passenger and transport ship.
- Sank in 1878 in Bass Strait, leaving only two survivors.

WRECKS FROM THE EARLY 1900s

Yongala

- A coastal transport ship.
- Sank in 1911.

HMAS Australia

- An Australian Navy flagship that was scuttled off the coast of Sydney in 1924.
- The largest shipwreck in Australian waters.

HMAS Australia

WRECKS FROM WORLD WAR II

USS Peary

HMAS Sydney

HMAS Sydney

- Sank with a loss of all on board, following a battle with the German ship Kormoran in 1941.
- Both wrecks lie off Shark Bay on the Western Australian coast.

M24

- A Japanese midget submarine.
- Sank in 1942 after its attack on Sydney Harbour during World War II.
- The submarine was discovered in 2006, along with the remains of its crew.

William Dawes

- A merchant vessel.
- Sank in 1942 off Tathra, New South Wales, after being torpedoed by a Japanese submarine during World War II.

Centaur

- A World War II hospital ship.
- Sank off Moreton Island, Queensland in 1943 after being torpedoed by a Japanese submarine.

Iron Knight

- An iron ore freighter.
- Sank in 1943 off Bermagui, New South Wales, after being torpedoed by a Japanese submarine during World War II.

USS Peary

- Sunk in Darwin Harbour in 1942 by Japanese bomber aircraft.

Historic shipwrecks are protected sites. Nothing can be taken from them and some are restricted zones because of their historical importance and fragility.

Centaur

Highest and Lowest

MOUNT KOSCIUSZKO

The highest place in Australia is Mount Kosciuszko. At 2,228 metres above sea level, the highest point in Australia is not really very high by world standards. People of normal fitness can take the track to the summit, covering a thirteen kilometre round trip from the town of Thredbo.

KATI THANDA / LAKE EYRE

Kati Thanda / Lake Eyre is a salt lake in the centre of Australia. On rare occasions it floods with water coming from rivers further north, creating an extensive wetland. Birds from thousands of kilometres away somehow find out that the temporary wetland exists, and thousands of them migrate there to feed on the fish, frogs, insects and crustaceans whose numbers explode in and around the lake. Kati Thanda / Lake Eyre is fifteen metres below sea level, making it the lowest place in Australia.

Glossary

algae aquatic plants without roots or flowers

crustacean type of aquatic invertebrate e.g. shrimps

dormant sleeping

erosion wearing away of rocks or parts of a landscape by wind or water

fibreglass construction material made of glass fibres

GPS Global Positioning System

lava molten rock that comes to the surface

millennia thousands of years

Morse Code code of dots and dashes, used to send messages by telegraph

mutineer sailor who takes over a ship by force

protea type of plant with nectar-rich flowers

salinity saltiness

savannah grasslands

scuttle sink a ship which is no longer needed

stalactites structures that form from the ceilings of caves by dripping calcium-rich water

stalagmites structures that form from the floors of caves from dripping calcium-rich water

stump part of a tree trunk left after the tree is cut down

tectonic plates large pieces of the Earth's crust that move

transpiration loss of water through leaves

Index